# THIS BOOK BELONGS TO:

| CONTACT INFORMATION | |
|---|---|
| NAME | |
| ADDRESS | |
| PHONE # | |
| EMAIL | |

Copyright © Teresa Rother
All rights reserved. No part of this publication may be reproduced, distributed, or transmitted in any form or by any means, including photocopy, recording, or other electronic or mechanical methods.

# DEDICATION

This Homeschool Log Book is dedicated to homeschoolers who want to keep accurate records and retain information for homeschool hours.

You are my inspiration for producing this book and I'm honored to be a part of helping you manage and retain important information regarding your education.

# HOW TO USE THIS BOOK

This Homeschool Log Book will help you record, collect, and organize your information in an easy to use format.

Here are examples of information for you to fill in and write the details for your daily schedule.

Fill in the following information:

1. Student Name - Write the student's name.
2. Week Of - Record weekly dates.
3. Subject - Fill in the subject.
4. Start Time - Record start time.
5. End Time - Record end time.
6. Notes - Use this space to jot down lesson plan notes, special assignments, upcoming tests, books to read, and other important information.

# HOMESCHOOL HOURS LOG BOOK

| STUDENT NAME: | | WEEK OF: | |
|---|---|---|---|

| SUBJECT | MONDAY | | TUESDAY | | WEDNESDAY | | THURSDAY | | FRIDAY | |
|---|---|---|---|---|---|---|---|---|---|---|
| | START | END | START | END | START | END | START | END | START | END |
| | | | | | | | | | | |
| | | | | | | | | | | |
| | | | | | | | | | | |
| | | | | | | | | | | |
| | | | | | | | | | | |
| | | | | | | | | | | |
| | | | | | | | | | | |
| | | | | | | | | | | |
| | | | | | | | | | | |
| | | | | | | | | | | |
| | | | | | | | | | | |
| | | | | | | | | | | |
| | | | | | | | | | | |

## NOTES

# HOMESCHOOL HOURS LOG BOOK

| STUDENT NAME: | | WEEK OF: | |

| SUBJECT | MONDAY | | TUESDAY | | WEDNESDAY | | THURSDAY | | FRIDAY | |
|---|---|---|---|---|---|---|---|---|---|---|
| | START | END | START | END | START | END | START | END | START | END |
| | | | | | | | | | | |
| | | | | | | | | | | |
| | | | | | | | | | | |
| | | | | | | | | | | |
| | | | | | | | | | | |
| | | | | | | | | | | |
| | | | | | | | | | | |
| | | | | | | | | | | |
| | | | | | | | | | | |
| | | | | | | | | | | |
| | | | | | | | | | | |
| | | | | | | | | | | |
| | | | | | | | | | | |

## NOTES

# HOMESCHOOL HOURS LOG BOOK

| STUDENT NAME: | | WEEK OF: | |
|---|---|---|---|

| SUBJECT | MONDAY | | TUESDAY | | WEDNESDAY | | THURSDAY | | FRIDAY | |
|---|---|---|---|---|---|---|---|---|---|---|
| | START | END | START | END | START | END | START | END | START | END |
| | | | | | | | | | | |
| | | | | | | | | | | |
| | | | | | | | | | | |
| | | | | | | | | | | |
| | | | | | | | | | | |
| | | | | | | | | | | |
| | | | | | | | | | | |
| | | | | | | | | | | |
| | | | | | | | | | | |
| | | | | | | | | | | |
| | | | | | | | | | | |
| | | | | | | | | | | |
| | | | | | | | | | | |

## NOTES

# HOMESCHOOL HOURS LOG BOOK

| STUDENT NAME: | | WEEK OF: | |
|---|---|---|---|

| SUBJECT | MONDAY | | TUESDAY | | WEDNESDAY | | THURSDAY | | FRIDAY | |
|---|---|---|---|---|---|---|---|---|---|---|
| | START | END | START | END | START | END | START | END | START | END |
| | | | | | | | | | | |
| | | | | | | | | | | |
| | | | | | | | | | | |
| | | | | | | | | | | |
| | | | | | | | | | | |
| | | | | | | | | | | |
| | | | | | | | | | | |
| | | | | | | | | | | |
| | | | | | | | | | | |
| | | | | | | | | | | |
| | | | | | | | | | | |
| | | | | | | | | | | |
| | | | | | | | | | | |

## NOTES

# HOMESCHOOL HOURS LOG BOOK

| STUDENT NAME: | | WEEK OF: | |

| SUBJECT | MONDAY | | TUESDAY | | WEDNESDAY | | THURSDAY | | FRIDAY | |
|---|---|---|---|---|---|---|---|---|---|---|
| | START | END | START | END | START | END | START | END | START | END |
| | | | | | | | | | | |
| | | | | | | | | | | |
| | | | | | | | | | | |
| | | | | | | | | | | |
| | | | | | | | | | | |
| | | | | | | | | | | |
| | | | | | | | | | | |
| | | | | | | | | | | |
| | | | | | | | | | | |
| | | | | | | | | | | |
| | | | | | | | | | | |
| | | | | | | | | | | |
| | | | | | | | | | | |

## NOTES

# HOMESCHOOL HOURS LOG BOOK

| STUDENT NAME: | | WEEK OF: | |

| SUBJECT | MONDAY | | TUESDAY | | WEDNESDAY | | THURSDAY | | FRIDAY | |
|---|---|---|---|---|---|---|---|---|---|---|
| | START | END | START | END | START | END | START | END | START | END |
| | | | | | | | | | | |
| | | | | | | | | | | |
| | | | | | | | | | | |
| | | | | | | | | | | |
| | | | | | | | | | | |
| | | | | | | | | | | |
| | | | | | | | | | | |
| | | | | | | | | | | |
| | | | | | | | | | | |
| | | | | | | | | | | |
| | | | | | | | | | | |
| | | | | | | | | | | |
| | | | | | | | | | | |

## NOTES

# HOMESCHOOL HOURS LOG BOOK

| STUDENT NAME: | | WEEK OF: | |
|---|---|---|---|

| SUBJECT | MONDAY | | TUESDAY | | WEDNESDAY | | THURSDAY | | FRIDAY | |
|---|---|---|---|---|---|---|---|---|---|---|
| | START | END | START | END | START | END | START | END | START | END |
| | | | | | | | | | | |
| | | | | | | | | | | |
| | | | | | | | | | | |
| | | | | | | | | | | |
| | | | | | | | | | | |
| | | | | | | | | | | |
| | | | | | | | | | | |
| | | | | | | | | | | |
| | | | | | | | | | | |
| | | | | | | | | | | |
| | | | | | | | | | | |
| | | | | | | | | | | |
| | | | | | | | | | | |

## NOTES

# HOMESCHOOL HOURS LOG BOOK

| STUDENT NAME: | | WEEK OF: | |
|---|---|---|---|

| SUBJECT | MONDAY | | TUESDAY | | WEDNESDAY | | THURSDAY | | FRIDAY | |
|---|---|---|---|---|---|---|---|---|---|---|
| | START | END | START | END | START | END | START | END | START | END |
| | | | | | | | | | | |
| | | | | | | | | | | |
| | | | | | | | | | | |
| | | | | | | | | | | |
| | | | | | | | | | | |
| | | | | | | | | | | |
| | | | | | | | | | | |
| | | | | | | | | | | |
| | | | | | | | | | | |
| | | | | | | | | | | |
| | | | | | | | | | | |
| | | | | | | | | | | |
| | | | | | | | | | | |

## NOTES

# HOMESCHOOL HOURS LOG BOOK

| STUDENT NAME: | | WEEK OF: | |
|---|---|---|---|

| SUBJECT | MONDAY | | TUESDAY | | WEDNESDAY | | THURSDAY | | FRIDAY | |
|---|---|---|---|---|---|---|---|---|---|---|
| | START | END | START | END | START | END | START | END | START | END |
| | | | | | | | | | | |
| | | | | | | | | | | |
| | | | | | | | | | | |
| | | | | | | | | | | |
| | | | | | | | | | | |
| | | | | | | | | | | |
| | | | | | | | | | | |
| | | | | | | | | | | |
| | | | | | | | | | | |
| | | | | | | | | | | |
| | | | | | | | | | | |
| | | | | | | | | | | |
| | | | | | | | | | | |

## NOTES

# HOMESCHOOL HOURS LOG BOOK

| STUDENT NAME: | | WEEK OF: | |

| SUBJECT | MONDAY | | TUESDAY | | WEDNESDAY | | THURSDAY | | FRIDAY | |
|---|---|---|---|---|---|---|---|---|---|---|
| | START | END | START | END | START | END | START | END | START | END |
| | | | | | | | | | | |
| | | | | | | | | | | |
| | | | | | | | | | | |
| | | | | | | | | | | |
| | | | | | | | | | | |
| | | | | | | | | | | |
| | | | | | | | | | | |
| | | | | | | | | | | |
| | | | | | | | | | | |
| | | | | | | | | | | |
| | | | | | | | | | | |
| | | | | | | | | | | |
| | | | | | | | | | | |

## NOTES

# HOMESCHOOL HOURS LOG BOOK

| STUDENT NAME: | | WEEK OF: | |

| SUBJECT | MONDAY | | TUESDAY | | WEDNESDAY | | THURSDAY | | FRIDAY | |
|---|---|---|---|---|---|---|---|---|---|---|
| | START | END | START | END | START | END | START | END | START | END |
| | | | | | | | | | | |
| | | | | | | | | | | |
| | | | | | | | | | | |
| | | | | | | | | | | |
| | | | | | | | | | | |
| | | | | | | | | | | |
| | | | | | | | | | | |
| | | | | | | | | | | |
| | | | | | | | | | | |
| | | | | | | | | | | |
| | | | | | | | | | | |
| | | | | | | | | | | |
| | | | | | | | | | | |

## NOTES

# HOMESCHOOL HOURS LOG BOOK

| STUDENT NAME: | | WEEK OF: | |

| SUBJECT | MONDAY | | TUESDAY | | WEDNESDAY | | THURSDAY | | FRIDAY | |
|---|---|---|---|---|---|---|---|---|---|---|
| | START | END | START | END | START | END | START | END | START | END |
| | | | | | | | | | | |
| | | | | | | | | | | |
| | | | | | | | | | | |
| | | | | | | | | | | |
| | | | | | | | | | | |
| | | | | | | | | | | |
| | | | | | | | | | | |
| | | | | | | | | | | |
| | | | | | | | | | | |
| | | | | | | | | | | |
| | | | | | | | | | | |
| | | | | | | | | | | |
| | | | | | | | | | | |

## NOTES

# HOMESCHOOL HOURS LOG BOOK

| STUDENT NAME: | | WEEK OF: | |
|---|---|---|---|

| SUBJECT | MONDAY | | TUESDAY | | WEDNESDAY | | THURSDAY | | FRIDAY | |
|---|---|---|---|---|---|---|---|---|---|---|
| | START | END | START | END | START | END | START | END | START | END |
| | | | | | | | | | | |
| | | | | | | | | | | |
| | | | | | | | | | | |
| | | | | | | | | | | |
| | | | | | | | | | | |
| | | | | | | | | | | |
| | | | | | | | | | | |
| | | | | | | | | | | |
| | | | | | | | | | | |
| | | | | | | | | | | |
| | | | | | | | | | | |
| | | | | | | | | | | |

## NOTES

# HOMESCHOOL HOURS LOG BOOK

| STUDENT NAME: | | WEEK OF: | |
|---|---|---|---|

| SUBJECT | MONDAY | | TUESDAY | | WEDNESDAY | | THURSDAY | | FRIDAY | |
|---|---|---|---|---|---|---|---|---|---|---|
| | START | END | START | END | START | END | START | END | START | END |
| | | | | | | | | | | |
| | | | | | | | | | | |
| | | | | | | | | | | |
| | | | | | | | | | | |
| | | | | | | | | | | |
| | | | | | | | | | | |
| | | | | | | | | | | |
| | | | | | | | | | | |
| | | | | | | | | | | |
| | | | | | | | | | | |
| | | | | | | | | | | |
| | | | | | | | | | | |
| | | | | | | | | | | |

## NOTES

# HOMESCHOOL HOURS LOG BOOK

| STUDENT NAME: | | WEEK OF: | |

| SUBJECT | MONDAY | | TUESDAY | | WEDNESDAY | | THURSDAY | | FRIDAY | |
|---|---|---|---|---|---|---|---|---|---|---|
| | START | END | START | END | START | END | START | END | START | END |
| | | | | | | | | | | |
| | | | | | | | | | | |
| | | | | | | | | | | |
| | | | | | | | | | | |
| | | | | | | | | | | |
| | | | | | | | | | | |
| | | | | | | | | | | |
| | | | | | | | | | | |
| | | | | | | | | | | |
| | | | | | | | | | | |
| | | | | | | | | | | |
| | | | | | | | | | | |

## NOTES

# HOMESCHOOL HOURS LOG BOOK

| STUDENT NAME: | | WEEK OF: | |
|---|---|---|---|

| SUBJECT | MONDAY | | TUESDAY | | WEDNESDAY | | THURSDAY | | FRIDAY | |
|---|---|---|---|---|---|---|---|---|---|---|
| | START | END | START | END | START | END | START | END | START | END |
| | | | | | | | | | | |
| | | | | | | | | | | |
| | | | | | | | | | | |
| | | | | | | | | | | |
| | | | | | | | | | | |
| | | | | | | | | | | |
| | | | | | | | | | | |
| | | | | | | | | | | |
| | | | | | | | | | | |
| | | | | | | | | | | |
| | | | | | | | | | | |
| | | | | | | | | | | |
| | | | | | | | | | | |

## NOTES

# HOMESCHOOL HOURS LOG BOOK

| STUDENT NAME: | | WEEK OF: | |
|---|---|---|---|

| SUBJECT | MONDAY | | TUESDAY | | WEDNESDAY | | THURSDAY | | FRIDAY | |
|---|---|---|---|---|---|---|---|---|---|---|
| | START | END | START | END | START | END | START | END | START | END |
| | | | | | | | | | | |
| | | | | | | | | | | |
| | | | | | | | | | | |
| | | | | | | | | | | |
| | | | | | | | | | | |
| | | | | | | | | | | |
| | | | | | | | | | | |
| | | | | | | | | | | |
| | | | | | | | | | | |
| | | | | | | | | | | |
| | | | | | | | | | | |
| | | | | | | | | | | |
| | | | | | | | | | | |

## NOTES

# HOMESCHOOL HOURS LOG BOOK

| STUDENT NAME: | | WEEK OF: | |

| SUBJECT | MONDAY | | TUESDAY | | WEDNESDAY | | THURSDAY | | FRIDAY | |
|---|---|---|---|---|---|---|---|---|---|---|
| | START | END | START | END | START | END | START | END | START | END |
| | | | | | | | | | | |
| | | | | | | | | | | |
| | | | | | | | | | | |
| | | | | | | | | | | |
| | | | | | | | | | | |
| | | | | | | | | | | |
| | | | | | | | | | | |
| | | | | | | | | | | |
| | | | | | | | | | | |
| | | | | | | | | | | |
| | | | | | | | | | | |
| | | | | | | | | | | |
| | | | | | | | | | | |

## NOTES

# HOMESCHOOL HOURS LOG BOOK

| STUDENT NAME: | | WEEK OF: | |
|---|---|---|---|

| SUBJECT | MONDAY | | TUESDAY | | WEDNESDAY | | THURSDAY | | FRIDAY | |
|---|---|---|---|---|---|---|---|---|---|---|
| | START | END | START | END | START | END | START | END | START | END |
| | | | | | | | | | | |
| | | | | | | | | | | |
| | | | | | | | | | | |
| | | | | | | | | | | |
| | | | | | | | | | | |
| | | | | | | | | | | |
| | | | | | | | | | | |
| | | | | | | | | | | |
| | | | | | | | | | | |
| | | | | | | | | | | |
| | | | | | | | | | | |
| | | | | | | | | | | |
| | | | | | | | | | | |

## NOTES

# HOMESCHOOL HOURS LOG BOOK

| STUDENT NAME: | | WEEK OF: | |
|---|---|---|---|

| SUBJECT | MONDAY | | TUESDAY | | WEDNESDAY | | THURSDAY | | FRIDAY | |
|---|---|---|---|---|---|---|---|---|---|---|
| | START | END | START | END | START | END | START | END | START | END |
| | | | | | | | | | | |
| | | | | | | | | | | |
| | | | | | | | | | | |
| | | | | | | | | | | |
| | | | | | | | | | | |
| | | | | | | | | | | |
| | | | | | | | | | | |
| | | | | | | | | | | |
| | | | | | | | | | | |
| | | | | | | | | | | |
| | | | | | | | | | | |
| | | | | | | | | | | |
| | | | | | | | | | | |

## NOTES

# HOMESCHOOL HOURS LOG BOOK

| STUDENT NAME: | | WEEK OF: | |

| SUBJECT | MONDAY | | TUESDAY | | WEDNESDAY | | THURSDAY | | FRIDAY | |
|---|---|---|---|---|---|---|---|---|---|---|
| | START | END | START | END | START | END | START | END | START | END |
| | | | | | | | | | | |
| | | | | | | | | | | |
| | | | | | | | | | | |
| | | | | | | | | | | |
| | | | | | | | | | | |
| | | | | | | | | | | |
| | | | | | | | | | | |
| | | | | | | | | | | |
| | | | | | | | | | | |
| | | | | | | | | | | |
| | | | | | | | | | | |
| | | | | | | | | | | |

## NOTES

# HOMESCHOOL HOURS LOG BOOK

| STUDENT NAME: | | WEEK OF: | |
|---|---|---|---|

| SUBJECT | MONDAY | | TUESDAY | | WEDNESDAY | | THURSDAY | | FRIDAY | |
|---|---|---|---|---|---|---|---|---|---|---|
| | START | END | START | END | START | END | START | END | START | END |
| | | | | | | | | | | |
| | | | | | | | | | | |
| | | | | | | | | | | |
| | | | | | | | | | | |
| | | | | | | | | | | |
| | | | | | | | | | | |
| | | | | | | | | | | |
| | | | | | | | | | | |
| | | | | | | | | | | |
| | | | | | | | | | | |
| | | | | | | | | | | |
| | | | | | | | | | | |
| | | | | | | | | | | |

## NOTES

# HOMESCHOOL HOURS LOG BOOK

| STUDENT NAME: | | WEEK OF: | |

| SUBJECT | MONDAY | | TUESDAY | | WEDNESDAY | | THURSDAY | | FRIDAY | |
|---|---|---|---|---|---|---|---|---|---|---|
| | START | END | START | END | START | END | START | END | START | END |
| | | | | | | | | | | |
| | | | | | | | | | | |
| | | | | | | | | | | |
| | | | | | | | | | | |
| | | | | | | | | | | |
| | | | | | | | | | | |
| | | | | | | | | | | |
| | | | | | | | | | | |
| | | | | | | | | | | |
| | | | | | | | | | | |
| | | | | | | | | | | |
| | | | | | | | | | | |
| | | | | | | | | | | |

## NOTES

# HOMESCHOOL HOURS LOG BOOK

| STUDENT NAME: | | WEEK OF: | |

| SUBJECT | MONDAY | | TUESDAY | | WEDNESDAY | | THURSDAY | | FRIDAY | |
|---|---|---|---|---|---|---|---|---|---|---|
| | START | END | START | END | START | END | START | END | START | END |
| | | | | | | | | | | |
| | | | | | | | | | | |
| | | | | | | | | | | |
| | | | | | | | | | | |
| | | | | | | | | | | |
| | | | | | | | | | | |
| | | | | | | | | | | |
| | | | | | | | | | | |
| | | | | | | | | | | |
| | | | | | | | | | | |
| | | | | | | | | | | |
| | | | | | | | | | | |
| | | | | | | | | | | |

## NOTES

# HOMESCHOOL HOURS LOG BOOK

| STUDENT NAME: | | WEEK OF: | |

| SUBJECT | MONDAY | | TUESDAY | | WEDNESDAY | | THURSDAY | | FRIDAY | |
|---|---|---|---|---|---|---|---|---|---|---|
| | START | END | START | END | START | END | START | END | START | END |
| | | | | | | | | | | |
| | | | | | | | | | | |
| | | | | | | | | | | |
| | | | | | | | | | | |
| | | | | | | | | | | |
| | | | | | | | | | | |
| | | | | | | | | | | |
| | | | | | | | | | | |
| | | | | | | | | | | |
| | | | | | | | | | | |
| | | | | | | | | | | |
| | | | | | | | | | | |
| | | | | | | | | | | |

## NOTES

# HOMESCHOOL HOURS LOG BOOK

| STUDENT NAME: | | WEEK OF: | |
|---|---|---|---|

| SUBJECT | MONDAY | | TUESDAY | | WEDNESDAY | | THURSDAY | | FRIDAY | |
|---|---|---|---|---|---|---|---|---|---|---|
| | START | END | START | END | START | END | START | END | START | END |
| | | | | | | | | | | |
| | | | | | | | | | | |
| | | | | | | | | | | |
| | | | | | | | | | | |
| | | | | | | | | | | |
| | | | | | | | | | | |
| | | | | | | | | | | |
| | | | | | | | | | | |
| | | | | | | | | | | |
| | | | | | | | | | | |
| | | | | | | | | | | |
| | | | | | | | | | | |
| | | | | | | | | | | |

## NOTES

# HOMESCHOOL HOURS LOG BOOK

| STUDENT NAME: | | WEEK OF: | |

| SUBJECT | MONDAY | | TUESDAY | | WEDNESDAY | | THURSDAY | | FRIDAY | |
|---|---|---|---|---|---|---|---|---|---|---|
| | START | END | START | END | START | END | START | END | START | END |
| | | | | | | | | | | |
| | | | | | | | | | | |
| | | | | | | | | | | |
| | | | | | | | | | | |
| | | | | | | | | | | |
| | | | | | | | | | | |
| | | | | | | | | | | |
| | | | | | | | | | | |
| | | | | | | | | | | |
| | | | | | | | | | | |
| | | | | | | | | | | |
| | | | | | | | | | | |
| | | | | | | | | | | |

## NOTES

# HOMESCHOOL HOURS LOG BOOK

| STUDENT NAME: | | WEEK OF: | |
|---|---|---|---|

| SUBJECT | MONDAY | | TUESDAY | | WEDNESDAY | | THURSDAY | | FRIDAY | |
|---|---|---|---|---|---|---|---|---|---|---|
| | START | END | START | END | START | END | START | END | START | END |
| | | | | | | | | | | |
| | | | | | | | | | | |
| | | | | | | | | | | |
| | | | | | | | | | | |
| | | | | | | | | | | |
| | | | | | | | | | | |
| | | | | | | | | | | |
| | | | | | | | | | | |
| | | | | | | | | | | |
| | | | | | | | | | | |
| | | | | | | | | | | |
| | | | | | | | | | | |
| | | | | | | | | | | |

## NOTES

# HOMESCHOOL HOURS LOG BOOK

| STUDENT NAME: | | WEEK OF: | |

| SUBJECT | MONDAY | | TUESDAY | | WEDNESDAY | | THURSDAY | | FRIDAY | |
|---|---|---|---|---|---|---|---|---|---|---|
| | START | END | START | END | START | END | START | END | START | END |
| | | | | | | | | | | |
| | | | | | | | | | | |
| | | | | | | | | | | |
| | | | | | | | | | | |
| | | | | | | | | | | |
| | | | | | | | | | | |
| | | | | | | | | | | |
| | | | | | | | | | | |
| | | | | | | | | | | |
| | | | | | | | | | | |
| | | | | | | | | | | |
| | | | | | | | | | | |
| | | | | | | | | | | |

## NOTES

# HOMESCHOOL HOURS LOG BOOK

| STUDENT NAME: | | WEEK OF: | |
|---|---|---|---|

| SUBJECT | MONDAY | | TUESDAY | | WEDNESDAY | | THURSDAY | | FRIDAY | |
|---|---|---|---|---|---|---|---|---|---|---|
| | START | END | START | END | START | END | START | END | START | END |
| | | | | | | | | | | |
| | | | | | | | | | | |
| | | | | | | | | | | |
| | | | | | | | | | | |
| | | | | | | | | | | |
| | | | | | | | | | | |
| | | | | | | | | | | |
| | | | | | | | | | | |
| | | | | | | | | | | |
| | | | | | | | | | | |
| | | | | | | | | | | |
| | | | | | | | | | | |
| | | | | | | | | | | |

## NOTES

# HOMESCHOOL HOURS LOG BOOK

| STUDENT NAME: | | WEEK OF: | |

| SUBJECT | MONDAY | | TUESDAY | | WEDNESDAY | | THURSDAY | | FRIDAY | |
|---|---|---|---|---|---|---|---|---|---|---|
| | START | END | START | END | START | END | START | END | START | END |
| | | | | | | | | | | |
| | | | | | | | | | | |
| | | | | | | | | | | |
| | | | | | | | | | | |
| | | | | | | | | | | |
| | | | | | | | | | | |
| | | | | | | | | | | |
| | | | | | | | | | | |
| | | | | | | | | | | |
| | | | | | | | | | | |
| | | | | | | | | | | |
| | | | | | | | | | | |
| | | | | | | | | | | |

## NOTES

# HOMESCHOOL HOURS LOG BOOK

| STUDENT NAME: | | | | | | | WEEK OF: | | | |
|---|---|---|---|---|---|---|---|---|---|---|

| SUBJECT | MONDAY | | TUESDAY | | WEDNESDAY | | THURSDAY | | FRIDAY | |
|---|---|---|---|---|---|---|---|---|---|---|
| | START | END | START | END | START | END | START | END | START | END |
| | | | | | | | | | | |
| | | | | | | | | | | |
| | | | | | | | | | | |
| | | | | | | | | | | |
| | | | | | | | | | | |
| | | | | | | | | | | |
| | | | | | | | | | | |
| | | | | | | | | | | |
| | | | | | | | | | | |
| | | | | | | | | | | |
| | | | | | | | | | | |
| | | | | | | | | | | |
| | | | | | | | | | | |

## NOTES

# HOMESCHOOL HOURS LOG BOOK

| STUDENT NAME: | | WEEK OF: | |

| SUBJECT | MONDAY | | TUESDAY | | WEDNESDAY | | THURSDAY | | FRIDAY | |
|---|---|---|---|---|---|---|---|---|---|---|
| | START | END | START | END | START | END | START | END | START | END |
| | | | | | | | | | | |
| | | | | | | | | | | |
| | | | | | | | | | | |
| | | | | | | | | | | |
| | | | | | | | | | | |
| | | | | | | | | | | |
| | | | | | | | | | | |
| | | | | | | | | | | |
| | | | | | | | | | | |
| | | | | | | | | | | |
| | | | | | | | | | | |
| | | | | | | | | | | |
| | | | | | | | | | | |

## NOTES

# HOMESCHOOL HOURS LOG BOOK

| STUDENT NAME: | | WEEK OF: | |
|---|---|---|---|

| SUBJECT | MONDAY | | TUESDAY | | WEDNESDAY | | THURSDAY | | FRIDAY | |
|---|---|---|---|---|---|---|---|---|---|---|
| | START | END | START | END | START | END | START | END | START | END |
| | | | | | | | | | | |
| | | | | | | | | | | |
| | | | | | | | | | | |
| | | | | | | | | | | |
| | | | | | | | | | | |
| | | | | | | | | | | |
| | | | | | | | | | | |
| | | | | | | | | | | |
| | | | | | | | | | | |
| | | | | | | | | | | |
| | | | | | | | | | | |
| | | | | | | | | | | |
| | | | | | | | | | | |

## NOTES

# HOMESCHOOL HOURS LOG BOOK

| STUDENT NAME: | | WEEK OF: | |

| SUBJECT | MONDAY | | TUESDAY | | WEDNESDAY | | THURSDAY | | FRIDAY | |
|---|---|---|---|---|---|---|---|---|---|---|
| | START | END | START | END | START | END | START | END | START | END |
| | | | | | | | | | | |
| | | | | | | | | | | |
| | | | | | | | | | | |
| | | | | | | | | | | |
| | | | | | | | | | | |
| | | | | | | | | | | |
| | | | | | | | | | | |
| | | | | | | | | | | |
| | | | | | | | | | | |
| | | | | | | | | | | |
| | | | | | | | | | | |
| | | | | | | | | | | |

## NOTES

# HOMESCHOOL HOURS LOG BOOK

| STUDENT NAME: | | | WEEK OF: | |
|---|---|---|---|---|

| SUBJECT | MONDAY | | TUESDAY | | WEDNESDAY | | THURSDAY | | FRIDAY | |
|---|---|---|---|---|---|---|---|---|---|---|
| | START | END | START | END | START | END | START | END | START | END |
| | | | | | | | | | | |
| | | | | | | | | | | |
| | | | | | | | | | | |
| | | | | | | | | | | |
| | | | | | | | | | | |
| | | | | | | | | | | |
| | | | | | | | | | | |
| | | | | | | | | | | |
| | | | | | | | | | | |
| | | | | | | | | | | |
| | | | | | | | | | | |
| | | | | | | | | | | |
| | | | | | | | | | | |

## NOTES

# HOMESCHOOL HOURS LOG BOOK

| STUDENT NAME: | | WEEK OF: | |

| SUBJECT | MONDAY | | TUESDAY | | WEDNESDAY | | THURSDAY | | FRIDAY | |
|---|---|---|---|---|---|---|---|---|---|---|
| | START | END | START | END | START | END | START | END | START | END |
| | | | | | | | | | | |
| | | | | | | | | | | |
| | | | | | | | | | | |
| | | | | | | | | | | |
| | | | | | | | | | | |
| | | | | | | | | | | |
| | | | | | | | | | | |
| | | | | | | | | | | |
| | | | | | | | | | | |
| | | | | | | | | | | |
| | | | | | | | | | | |
| | | | | | | | | | | |
| | | | | | | | | | | |

## NOTES

# HOMESCHOOL HOURS LOG BOOK

| STUDENT NAME: | | WEEK OF: | |
|---|---|---|---|

| SUBJECT | MONDAY | | TUESDAY | | WEDNESDAY | | THURSDAY | | FRIDAY | |
|---|---|---|---|---|---|---|---|---|---|---|
| | START | END | START | END | START | END | START | END | START | END |
| | | | | | | | | | | |
| | | | | | | | | | | |
| | | | | | | | | | | |
| | | | | | | | | | | |
| | | | | | | | | | | |
| | | | | | | | | | | |
| | | | | | | | | | | |
| | | | | | | | | | | |
| | | | | | | | | | | |
| | | | | | | | | | | |
| | | | | | | | | | | |
| | | | | | | | | | | |
| | | | | | | | | | | |
| | | | | | | | | | | |

## NOTES

# HOMESCHOOL HOURS LOG BOOK

| STUDENT NAME: | | WEEK OF: | |

| SUBJECT | MONDAY | | TUESDAY | | WEDNESDAY | | THURSDAY | | FRIDAY | |
|---|---|---|---|---|---|---|---|---|---|---|
| | START | END | START | END | START | END | START | END | START | END |
| | | | | | | | | | | |
| | | | | | | | | | | |
| | | | | | | | | | | |
| | | | | | | | | | | |
| | | | | | | | | | | |
| | | | | | | | | | | |
| | | | | | | | | | | |
| | | | | | | | | | | |
| | | | | | | | | | | |
| | | | | | | | | | | |
| | | | | | | | | | | |
| | | | | | | | | | | |

## NOTES

# HOMESCHOOL HOURS LOG BOOK

| STUDENT NAME: | | WEEK OF: | |
|---|---|---|---|

| SUBJECT | MONDAY | | TUESDAY | | WEDNESDAY | | THURSDAY | | FRIDAY | |
|---|---|---|---|---|---|---|---|---|---|---|
| | START | END | START | END | START | END | START | END | START | END |
| | | | | | | | | | | |
| | | | | | | | | | | |
| | | | | | | | | | | |
| | | | | | | | | | | |
| | | | | | | | | | | |
| | | | | | | | | | | |
| | | | | | | | | | | |
| | | | | | | | | | | |
| | | | | | | | | | | |
| | | | | | | | | | | |
| | | | | | | | | | | |
| | | | | | | | | | | |
| | | | | | | | | | | |

## NOTES

# HOMESCHOOL HOURS LOG BOOK

| STUDENT NAME: | | WEEK OF: | |

| SUBJECT | MONDAY | | TUESDAY | | WEDNESDAY | | THURSDAY | | FRIDAY | |
|---|---|---|---|---|---|---|---|---|---|---|
| | START | END | START | END | START | END | START | END | START | END |
| | | | | | | | | | | |
| | | | | | | | | | | |
| | | | | | | | | | | |
| | | | | | | | | | | |
| | | | | | | | | | | |
| | | | | | | | | | | |
| | | | | | | | | | | |
| | | | | | | | | | | |
| | | | | | | | | | | |
| | | | | | | | | | | |
| | | | | | | | | | | |
| | | | | | | | | | | |
| | | | | | | | | | | |

## NOTES

# HOMESCHOOL HOURS LOG BOOK

| STUDENT NAME: | | WEEK OF: | |

| SUBJECT | MONDAY | | TUESDAY | | WEDNESDAY | | THURSDAY | | FRIDAY | |
|---|---|---|---|---|---|---|---|---|---|---|
| | START | END | START | END | START | END | START | END | START | END |
| | | | | | | | | | | |
| | | | | | | | | | | |
| | | | | | | | | | | |
| | | | | | | | | | | |
| | | | | | | | | | | |
| | | | | | | | | | | |
| | | | | | | | | | | |
| | | | | | | | | | | |
| | | | | | | | | | | |
| | | | | | | | | | | |
| | | | | | | | | | | |
| | | | | | | | | | | |
| | | | | | | | | | | |

## NOTES

# HOMESCHOOL HOURS LOG BOOK

| STUDENT NAME: | | WEEK OF: | |
|---|---|---|---|

| SUBJECT | MONDAY | | TUESDAY | | WEDNESDAY | | THURSDAY | | FRIDAY | |
|---|---|---|---|---|---|---|---|---|---|---|
| | START | END | START | END | START | END | START | END | START | END |
| | | | | | | | | | | |
| | | | | | | | | | | |
| | | | | | | | | | | |
| | | | | | | | | | | |
| | | | | | | | | | | |
| | | | | | | | | | | |
| | | | | | | | | | | |
| | | | | | | | | | | |
| | | | | | | | | | | |
| | | | | | | | | | | |
| | | | | | | | | | | |
| | | | | | | | | | | |
| | | | | | | | | | | |

## NOTES

# HOMESCHOOL HOURS LOG BOOK

| STUDENT NAME: | | WEEK OF: | |
|---|---|---|---|

| SUBJECT | MONDAY | | TUESDAY | | WEDNESDAY | | THURSDAY | | FRIDAY | |
|---|---|---|---|---|---|---|---|---|---|---|
| | START | END | START | END | START | END | START | END | START | END |
| | | | | | | | | | | |
| | | | | | | | | | | |
| | | | | | | | | | | |
| | | | | | | | | | | |
| | | | | | | | | | | |
| | | | | | | | | | | |
| | | | | | | | | | | |
| | | | | | | | | | | |
| | | | | | | | | | | |
| | | | | | | | | | | |
| | | | | | | | | | | |
| | | | | | | | | | | |
| | | | | | | | | | | |

## NOTES

# HOMESCHOOL HOURS LOG BOOK

| STUDENT NAME: | | WEEK OF: | |

| SUBJECT | MONDAY | | TUESDAY | | WEDNESDAY | | THURSDAY | | FRIDAY | |
|---|---|---|---|---|---|---|---|---|---|---|
| | START | END | START | END | START | END | START | END | START | END |
| | | | | | | | | | | |
| | | | | | | | | | | |
| | | | | | | | | | | |
| | | | | | | | | | | |
| | | | | | | | | | | |
| | | | | | | | | | | |
| | | | | | | | | | | |
| | | | | | | | | | | |
| | | | | | | | | | | |
| | | | | | | | | | | |
| | | | | | | | | | | |
| | | | | | | | | | | |
| | | | | | | | | | | |

## NOTES

# HOMESCHOOL HOURS LOG BOOK

| STUDENT NAME: | | WEEK OF: | |

| SUBJECT | MONDAY | | TUESDAY | | WEDNESDAY | | THURSDAY | | FRIDAY | |
|---|---|---|---|---|---|---|---|---|---|---|
| | START | END | START | END | START | END | START | END | START | END |
| | | | | | | | | | | |
| | | | | | | | | | | |
| | | | | | | | | | | |
| | | | | | | | | | | |
| | | | | | | | | | | |
| | | | | | | | | | | |
| | | | | | | | | | | |
| | | | | | | | | | | |
| | | | | | | | | | | |
| | | | | | | | | | | |
| | | | | | | | | | | |
| | | | | | | | | | | |
| | | | | | | | | | | |

## NOTES

# HOMESCHOOL HOURS LOG BOOK

| STUDENT NAME: | | WEEK OF: | |
|---|---|---|---|

| SUBJECT | MONDAY | | TUESDAY | | WEDNESDAY | | THURSDAY | | FRIDAY | |
|---|---|---|---|---|---|---|---|---|---|---|
| | START | END | START | END | START | END | START | END | START | END |
| | | | | | | | | | | |
| | | | | | | | | | | |
| | | | | | | | | | | |
| | | | | | | | | | | |
| | | | | | | | | | | |
| | | | | | | | | | | |
| | | | | | | | | | | |
| | | | | | | | | | | |
| | | | | | | | | | | |
| | | | | | | | | | | |
| | | | | | | | | | | |
| | | | | | | | | | | |
| | | | | | | | | | | |

## NOTES

# HOMESCHOOL HOURS LOG BOOK

| STUDENT NAME: | | WEEK OF: | |
|---|---|---|---|

| SUBJECT | MONDAY | | TUESDAY | | WEDNESDAY | | THURSDAY | | FRIDAY | |
|---|---|---|---|---|---|---|---|---|---|---|
| | START | END | START | END | START | END | START | END | START | END |
| | | | | | | | | | | |
| | | | | | | | | | | |
| | | | | | | | | | | |
| | | | | | | | | | | |
| | | | | | | | | | | |
| | | | | | | | | | | |
| | | | | | | | | | | |
| | | | | | | | | | | |
| | | | | | | | | | | |
| | | | | | | | | | | |
| | | | | | | | | | | |
| | | | | | | | | | | |
| | | | | | | | | | | |

## NOTES

# HOMESCHOOL HOURS LOG BOOK

| STUDENT NAME: | | WEEK OF: | |

| SUBJECT | MONDAY | | TUESDAY | | WEDNESDAY | | THURSDAY | | FRIDAY | |
|---|---|---|---|---|---|---|---|---|---|---|
| | START | END | START | END | START | END | START | END | START | END |
| | | | | | | | | | | |
| | | | | | | | | | | |
| | | | | | | | | | | |
| | | | | | | | | | | |
| | | | | | | | | | | |
| | | | | | | | | | | |
| | | | | | | | | | | |
| | | | | | | | | | | |
| | | | | | | | | | | |
| | | | | | | | | | | |
| | | | | | | | | | | |
| | | | | | | | | | | |
| | | | | | | | | | | |
| | | | | | | | | | | |

## NOTES

# HOMESCHOOL HOURS LOG BOOK

| STUDENT NAME: | | WEEK OF: | |
|---|---|---|---|

| SUBJECT | MONDAY | | TUESDAY | | WEDNESDAY | | THURSDAY | | FRIDAY | |
|---|---|---|---|---|---|---|---|---|---|---|
| | START | END | START | END | START | END | START | END | START | END |
| | | | | | | | | | | |
| | | | | | | | | | | |
| | | | | | | | | | | |
| | | | | | | | | | | |
| | | | | | | | | | | |
| | | | | | | | | | | |
| | | | | | | | | | | |
| | | | | | | | | | | |
| | | | | | | | | | | |
| | | | | | | | | | | |
| | | | | | | | | | | |
| | | | | | | | | | | |
| | | | | | | | | | | |

## NOTES

# HOMESCHOOL HOURS LOG BOOK

| STUDENT NAME: | | WEEK OF: | |
|---|---|---|---|

| SUBJECT | MONDAY | | TUESDAY | | WEDNESDAY | | THURSDAY | | FRIDAY | |
|---|---|---|---|---|---|---|---|---|---|---|
| | START | END | START | END | START | END | START | END | START | END |
| | | | | | | | | | | |
| | | | | | | | | | | |
| | | | | | | | | | | |
| | | | | | | | | | | |
| | | | | | | | | | | |
| | | | | | | | | | | |
| | | | | | | | | | | |
| | | | | | | | | | | |
| | | | | | | | | | | |
| | | | | | | | | | | |
| | | | | | | | | | | |
| | | | | | | | | | | |
| | | | | | | | | | | |

## NOTES

# HOMESCHOOL HOURS LOG BOOK

| STUDENT NAME: | | WEEK OF: | |
|---|---|---|---|

| SUBJECT | MONDAY | | TUESDAY | | WEDNESDAY | | THURSDAY | | FRIDAY | |
|---|---|---|---|---|---|---|---|---|---|---|
| | START | END | START | END | START | END | START | END | START | END |
| | | | | | | | | | | |
| | | | | | | | | | | |
| | | | | | | | | | | |
| | | | | | | | | | | |
| | | | | | | | | | | |
| | | | | | | | | | | |
| | | | | | | | | | | |
| | | | | | | | | | | |
| | | | | | | | | | | |
| | | | | | | | | | | |
| | | | | | | | | | | |
| | | | | | | | | | | |
| | | | | | | | | | | |

## NOTES

# HOMESCHOOL HOURS LOG BOOK

| STUDENT NAME: | | WEEK OF: | |

| SUBJECT | MONDAY | | TUESDAY | | WEDNESDAY | | THURSDAY | | FRIDAY | |
|---|---|---|---|---|---|---|---|---|---|---|
| | START | END | START | END | START | END | START | END | START | END |
| | | | | | | | | | | |
| | | | | | | | | | | |
| | | | | | | | | | | |
| | | | | | | | | | | |
| | | | | | | | | | | |
| | | | | | | | | | | |
| | | | | | | | | | | |
| | | | | | | | | | | |
| | | | | | | | | | | |
| | | | | | | | | | | |
| | | | | | | | | | | |
| | | | | | | | | | | |
| | | | | | | | | | | |

## NOTES

# HOMESCHOOL HOURS LOG BOOK

| STUDENT NAME: | | | | | WEEK OF: | | | | | |
|---|---|---|---|---|---|---|---|---|---|---|

| SUBJECT | MONDAY | | TUESDAY | | WEDNESDAY | | THURSDAY | | FRIDAY | |
|---|---|---|---|---|---|---|---|---|---|---|
| | START | END | START | END | START | END | START | END | START | END |
| | | | | | | | | | | |
| | | | | | | | | | | |
| | | | | | | | | | | |
| | | | | | | | | | | |
| | | | | | | | | | | |
| | | | | | | | | | | |
| | | | | | | | | | | |
| | | | | | | | | | | |
| | | | | | | | | | | |
| | | | | | | | | | | |
| | | | | | | | | | | |
| | | | | | | | | | | |
| | | | | | | | | | | |

## NOTES

# HOMESCHOOL HOURS LOG BOOK

| STUDENT NAME: | | WEEK OF: | |
|---|---|---|---|

| SUBJECT | MONDAY | | TUESDAY | | WEDNESDAY | | THURSDAY | | FRIDAY | |
|---|---|---|---|---|---|---|---|---|---|---|
| | START | END | START | END | START | END | START | END | START | END |
| | | | | | | | | | | |
| | | | | | | | | | | |
| | | | | | | | | | | |
| | | | | | | | | | | |
| | | | | | | | | | | |
| | | | | | | | | | | |
| | | | | | | | | | | |
| | | | | | | | | | | |
| | | | | | | | | | | |
| | | | | | | | | | | |
| | | | | | | | | | | |
| | | | | | | | | | | |

## NOTES

# HOMESCHOOL HOURS LOG BOOK

| STUDENT NAME: | | WEEK OF: | |

| SUBJECT | MONDAY | | TUESDAY | | WEDNESDAY | | THURSDAY | | FRIDAY | |
|---|---|---|---|---|---|---|---|---|---|---|
| | START | END | START | END | START | END | START | END | START | END |
| | | | | | | | | | | |
| | | | | | | | | | | |
| | | | | | | | | | | |
| | | | | | | | | | | |
| | | | | | | | | | | |
| | | | | | | | | | | |
| | | | | | | | | | | |
| | | | | | | | | | | |
| | | | | | | | | | | |
| | | | | | | | | | | |
| | | | | | | | | | | |
| | | | | | | | | | | |
| | | | | | | | | | | |

## NOTES

# HOMESCHOOL HOURS LOG BOOK

| STUDENT NAME: | | WEEK OF: | |

| SUBJECT | MONDAY | | TUESDAY | | WEDNESDAY | | THURSDAY | | FRIDAY | |
|---|---|---|---|---|---|---|---|---|---|---|
| | START | END | START | END | START | END | START | END | START | END |
| | | | | | | | | | | |
| | | | | | | | | | | |
| | | | | | | | | | | |
| | | | | | | | | | | |
| | | | | | | | | | | |
| | | | | | | | | | | |
| | | | | | | | | | | |
| | | | | | | | | | | |
| | | | | | | | | | | |
| | | | | | | | | | | |
| | | | | | | | | | | |
| | | | | | | | | | | |
| | | | | | | | | | | |

## NOTES

# HOMESCHOOL HOURS LOG BOOK

| STUDENT NAME: | | WEEK OF: | |
|---|---|---|---|

| SUBJECT | MONDAY | | TUESDAY | | WEDNESDAY | | THURSDAY | | FRIDAY | |
|---|---|---|---|---|---|---|---|---|---|---|
| | START | END | START | END | START | END | START | END | START | END |
| | | | | | | | | | | |
| | | | | | | | | | | |
| | | | | | | | | | | |
| | | | | | | | | | | |
| | | | | | | | | | | |
| | | | | | | | | | | |
| | | | | | | | | | | |
| | | | | | | | | | | |
| | | | | | | | | | | |
| | | | | | | | | | | |
| | | | | | | | | | | |
| | | | | | | | | | | |
| | | | | | | | | | | |

## NOTES

# HOMESCHOOL HOURS LOG BOOK

| STUDENT NAME: | | | WEEK OF: | |
|---|---|---|---|---|

| SUBJECT | MONDAY | | TUESDAY | | WEDNESDAY | | THURSDAY | | FRIDAY | |
|---|---|---|---|---|---|---|---|---|---|---|
| | START | END | START | END | START | END | START | END | START | END |
| | | | | | | | | | | |
| | | | | | | | | | | |
| | | | | | | | | | | |
| | | | | | | | | | | |
| | | | | | | | | | | |
| | | | | | | | | | | |
| | | | | | | | | | | |
| | | | | | | | | | | |
| | | | | | | | | | | |
| | | | | | | | | | | |
| | | | | | | | | | | |
| | | | | | | | | | | |
| | | | | | | | | | | |

## NOTES

# HOMESCHOOL HOURS LOG BOOK

| STUDENT NAME: | | WEEK OF: | |
|---|---|---|---|

| SUBJECT | MONDAY | | TUESDAY | | WEDNESDAY | | THURSDAY | | FRIDAY | |
|---|---|---|---|---|---|---|---|---|---|---|
| | START | END | START | END | START | END | START | END | START | END |
| | | | | | | | | | | |
| | | | | | | | | | | |
| | | | | | | | | | | |
| | | | | | | | | | | |
| | | | | | | | | | | |
| | | | | | | | | | | |
| | | | | | | | | | | |
| | | | | | | | | | | |
| | | | | | | | | | | |
| | | | | | | | | | | |
| | | | | | | | | | | |
| | | | | | | | | | | |
| | | | | | | | | | | |

## NOTES

# HOMESCHOOL HOURS LOG BOOK

| STUDENT NAME: | | | WEEK OF: | |
|---|---|---|---|---|

| SUBJECT | MONDAY | | TUESDAY | | WEDNESDAY | | THURSDAY | | FRIDAY | |
|---|---|---|---|---|---|---|---|---|---|---|
| | START | END | START | END | START | END | START | END | START | END |
| | | | | | | | | | | |
| | | | | | | | | | | |
| | | | | | | | | | | |
| | | | | | | | | | | |
| | | | | | | | | | | |
| | | | | | | | | | | |
| | | | | | | | | | | |
| | | | | | | | | | | |
| | | | | | | | | | | |
| | | | | | | | | | | |
| | | | | | | | | | | |
| | | | | | | | | | | |
| | | | | | | | | | | |

## NOTES

# HOMESCHOOL HOURS LOG BOOK

| STUDENT NAME: | | WEEK OF: | |
|---|---|---|---|

| SUBJECT | MONDAY | | TUESDAY | | WEDNESDAY | | THURSDAY | | FRIDAY | |
|---|---|---|---|---|---|---|---|---|---|---|
| | START | END | START | END | START | END | START | END | START | END |
| | | | | | | | | | | |
| | | | | | | | | | | |
| | | | | | | | | | | |
| | | | | | | | | | | |
| | | | | | | | | | | |
| | | | | | | | | | | |
| | | | | | | | | | | |
| | | | | | | | | | | |
| | | | | | | | | | | |
| | | | | | | | | | | |
| | | | | | | | | | | |
| | | | | | | | | | | |
| | | | | | | | | | | |

## NOTES

# HOMESCHOOL HOURS LOG BOOK

| STUDENT NAME: | | WEEK OF: | |

| SUBJECT | MONDAY | | TUESDAY | | WEDNESDAY | | THURSDAY | | FRIDAY | |
|---|---|---|---|---|---|---|---|---|---|---|
| | START | END | START | END | START | END | START | END | START | END |
| | | | | | | | | | | |
| | | | | | | | | | | |
| | | | | | | | | | | |
| | | | | | | | | | | |
| | | | | | | | | | | |
| | | | | | | | | | | |
| | | | | | | | | | | |
| | | | | | | | | | | |
| | | | | | | | | | | |
| | | | | | | | | | | |
| | | | | | | | | | | |
| | | | | | | | | | | |
| | | | | | | | | | | |

## NOTES

# HOMESCHOOL HOURS LOG BOOK

| STUDENT NAME: | | WEEK OF: | |

| SUBJECT | MONDAY | | TUESDAY | | WEDNESDAY | | THURSDAY | | FRIDAY | |
|---|---|---|---|---|---|---|---|---|---|---|
| | START | END | START | END | START | END | START | END | START | END |
| | | | | | | | | | | |
| | | | | | | | | | | |
| | | | | | | | | | | |
| | | | | | | | | | | |
| | | | | | | | | | | |
| | | | | | | | | | | |
| | | | | | | | | | | |
| | | | | | | | | | | |
| | | | | | | | | | | |
| | | | | | | | | | | |
| | | | | | | | | | | |
| | | | | | | | | | | |
| | | | | | | | | | | |

## NOTES

# HOMESCHOOL HOURS LOG BOOK

| STUDENT NAME: | | WEEK OF: | |

| SUBJECT | MONDAY | | TUESDAY | | WEDNESDAY | | THURSDAY | | FRIDAY | |
|---|---|---|---|---|---|---|---|---|---|---|
| | START | END | START | END | START | END | START | END | START | END |
| | | | | | | | | | | |
| | | | | | | | | | | |
| | | | | | | | | | | |
| | | | | | | | | | | |
| | | | | | | | | | | |
| | | | | | | | | | | |
| | | | | | | | | | | |
| | | | | | | | | | | |
| | | | | | | | | | | |
| | | | | | | | | | | |
| | | | | | | | | | | |
| | | | | | | | | | | |
| | | | | | | | | | | |

## NOTES

# HOMESCHOOL HOURS LOG BOOK

| STUDENT NAME: | | WEEK OF: | |
|---|---|---|---|

| SUBJECT | MONDAY | | TUESDAY | | WEDNESDAY | | THURSDAY | | FRIDAY | |
|---|---|---|---|---|---|---|---|---|---|---|
| | START | END | START | END | START | END | START | END | START | END |
| | | | | | | | | | | |
| | | | | | | | | | | |
| | | | | | | | | | | |
| | | | | | | | | | | |
| | | | | | | | | | | |
| | | | | | | | | | | |
| | | | | | | | | | | |
| | | | | | | | | | | |
| | | | | | | | | | | |
| | | | | | | | | | | |
| | | | | | | | | | | |
| | | | | | | | | | | |
| | | | | | | | | | | |

## NOTES

# HOMESCHOOL HOURS LOG BOOK

| STUDENT NAME: | | WEEK OF: | |
|---|---|---|---|

| SUBJECT | MONDAY | | TUESDAY | | WEDNESDAY | | THURSDAY | | FRIDAY | |
|---|---|---|---|---|---|---|---|---|---|---|
| | START | END | START | END | START | END | START | END | START | END |
| | | | | | | | | | | |
| | | | | | | | | | | |
| | | | | | | | | | | |
| | | | | | | | | | | |
| | | | | | | | | | | |
| | | | | | | | | | | |
| | | | | | | | | | | |
| | | | | | | | | | | |
| | | | | | | | | | | |
| | | | | | | | | | | |
| | | | | | | | | | | |
| | | | | | | | | | | |
| | | | | | | | | | | |
| | | | | | | | | | | |

## NOTES

# HOMESCHOOL HOURS LOG BOOK

| STUDENT NAME: | | WEEK OF: | |
|---|---|---|---|

| SUBJECT | MONDAY | | TUESDAY | | WEDNESDAY | | THURSDAY | | FRIDAY | |
|---|---|---|---|---|---|---|---|---|---|---|
| | START | END | START | END | START | END | START | END | START | END |
| | | | | | | | | | | |
| | | | | | | | | | | |
| | | | | | | | | | | |
| | | | | | | | | | | |
| | | | | | | | | | | |
| | | | | | | | | | | |
| | | | | | | | | | | |
| | | | | | | | | | | |
| | | | | | | | | | | |
| | | | | | | | | | | |
| | | | | | | | | | | |
| | | | | | | | | | | |
| | | | | | | | | | | |

## NOTES

# HOMESCHOOL HOURS LOG BOOK

| STUDENT NAME: | | WEEK OF: | |

| SUBJECT | MONDAY | | TUESDAY | | WEDNESDAY | | THURSDAY | | FRIDAY | |
|---|---|---|---|---|---|---|---|---|---|---|
| | START | END | START | END | START | END | START | END | START | END |
| | | | | | | | | | | |
| | | | | | | | | | | |
| | | | | | | | | | | |
| | | | | | | | | | | |
| | | | | | | | | | | |
| | | | | | | | | | | |
| | | | | | | | | | | |
| | | | | | | | | | | |
| | | | | | | | | | | |
| | | | | | | | | | | |
| | | | | | | | | | | |
| | | | | | | | | | | |
| | | | | | | | | | | |

## NOTES

# HOMESCHOOL HOURS LOG BOOK

| STUDENT NAME: | | WEEK OF: | |
|---|---|---|---|

| SUBJECT | MONDAY | | TUESDAY | | WEDNESDAY | | THURSDAY | | FRIDAY | |
|---|---|---|---|---|---|---|---|---|---|---|
| | START | END | START | END | START | END | START | END | START | END |
| | | | | | | | | | | |
| | | | | | | | | | | |
| | | | | | | | | | | |
| | | | | | | | | | | |
| | | | | | | | | | | |
| | | | | | | | | | | |
| | | | | | | | | | | |
| | | | | | | | | | | |
| | | | | | | | | | | |
| | | | | | | | | | | |
| | | | | | | | | | | |
| | | | | | | | | | | |
| | | | | | | | | | | |

## NOTES

# HOMESCHOOL HOURS LOG BOOK

| STUDENT NAME: | | WEEK OF: | |

| SUBJECT | MONDAY | | TUESDAY | | WEDNESDAY | | THURSDAY | | FRIDAY | |
|---|---|---|---|---|---|---|---|---|---|---|
| | START | END | START | END | START | END | START | END | START | END |
| | | | | | | | | | | |
| | | | | | | | | | | |
| | | | | | | | | | | |
| | | | | | | | | | | |
| | | | | | | | | | | |
| | | | | | | | | | | |
| | | | | | | | | | | |
| | | | | | | | | | | |
| | | | | | | | | | | |
| | | | | | | | | | | |
| | | | | | | | | | | |
| | | | | | | | | | | |
| | | | | | | | | | | |

## NOTES

# HOMESCHOOL HOURS LOG BOOK

| STUDENT NAME: | | WEEK OF: | |

| SUBJECT | MONDAY | | TUESDAY | | WEDNESDAY | | THURSDAY | | FRIDAY | |
|---|---|---|---|---|---|---|---|---|---|---|
| | START | END | START | END | START | END | START | END | START | END |
| | | | | | | | | | | |
| | | | | | | | | | | |
| | | | | | | | | | | |
| | | | | | | | | | | |
| | | | | | | | | | | |
| | | | | | | | | | | |
| | | | | | | | | | | |
| | | | | | | | | | | |
| | | | | | | | | | | |
| | | | | | | | | | | |
| | | | | | | | | | | |
| | | | | | | | | | | |
| | | | | | | | | | | |

## NOTES

# HOMESCHOOL HOURS LOG BOOK

| STUDENT NAME: | | WEEK OF: | |

| SUBJECT | MONDAY | | TUESDAY | | WEDNESDAY | | THURSDAY | | FRIDAY | |
|---|---|---|---|---|---|---|---|---|---|---|
| | START | END | START | END | START | END | START | END | START | END |
| | | | | | | | | | | |
| | | | | | | | | | | |
| | | | | | | | | | | |
| | | | | | | | | | | |
| | | | | | | | | | | |
| | | | | | | | | | | |
| | | | | | | | | | | |
| | | | | | | | | | | |
| | | | | | | | | | | |
| | | | | | | | | | | |
| | | | | | | | | | | |
| | | | | | | | | | | |
| | | | | | | | | | | |

## NOTES

# HOMESCHOOL HOURS LOG BOOK

| STUDENT NAME: | | WEEK OF: | |
|---|---|---|---|

| SUBJECT | MONDAY | | TUESDAY | | WEDNESDAY | | THURSDAY | | FRIDAY | |
|---|---|---|---|---|---|---|---|---|---|---|
| | START | END | START | END | START | END | START | END | START | END |
| | | | | | | | | | | |
| | | | | | | | | | | |
| | | | | | | | | | | |
| | | | | | | | | | | |
| | | | | | | | | | | |
| | | | | | | | | | | |
| | | | | | | | | | | |
| | | | | | | | | | | |
| | | | | | | | | | | |
| | | | | | | | | | | |
| | | | | | | | | | | |
| | | | | | | | | | | |
| | | | | | | | | | | |
| | | | | | | | | | | |

## NOTES

# HOMESCHOOL HOURS LOG BOOK

| STUDENT NAME: | | WEEK OF: | |
|---|---|---|---|

| SUBJECT | MONDAY | | TUESDAY | | WEDNESDAY | | THURSDAY | | FRIDAY | |
|---|---|---|---|---|---|---|---|---|---|---|
| | START | END | START | END | START | END | START | END | START | END |
| | | | | | | | | | | |
| | | | | | | | | | | |
| | | | | | | | | | | |
| | | | | | | | | | | |
| | | | | | | | | | | |
| | | | | | | | | | | |
| | | | | | | | | | | |
| | | | | | | | | | | |
| | | | | | | | | | | |
| | | | | | | | | | | |
| | | | | | | | | | | |
| | | | | | | | | | | |
| | | | | | | | | | | |

## NOTES

# HOMESCHOOL HOURS LOG BOOK

| STUDENT NAME: | | | WEEK OF: | |

| SUBJECT | MONDAY | | TUESDAY | | WEDNESDAY | | THURSDAY | | FRIDAY | |
|---|---|---|---|---|---|---|---|---|---|---|
| | START | END | START | END | START | END | START | END | START | END |
| | | | | | | | | | | |
| | | | | | | | | | | |
| | | | | | | | | | | |
| | | | | | | | | | | |
| | | | | | | | | | | |
| | | | | | | | | | | |
| | | | | | | | | | | |
| | | | | | | | | | | |
| | | | | | | | | | | |
| | | | | | | | | | | |
| | | | | | | | | | | |
| | | | | | | | | | | |
| | | | | | | | | | | |

## NOTES

# HOMESCHOOL HOURS LOG BOOK

| STUDENT NAME: | | WEEK OF: | |

| SUBJECT | MONDAY | | TUESDAY | | WEDNESDAY | | THURSDAY | | FRIDAY | |
|---|---|---|---|---|---|---|---|---|---|---|
| | START | END | START | END | START | END | START | END | START | END |
| | | | | | | | | | | |
| | | | | | | | | | | |
| | | | | | | | | | | |
| | | | | | | | | | | |
| | | | | | | | | | | |
| | | | | | | | | | | |
| | | | | | | | | | | |
| | | | | | | | | | | |
| | | | | | | | | | | |
| | | | | | | | | | | |
| | | | | | | | | | | |
| | | | | | | | | | | |
| | | | | | | | | | | |

## NOTES

# HOMESCHOOL HOURS LOG BOOK

| STUDENT NAME: | | | WEEK OF: | |
|---|---|---|---|---|

| SUBJECT | MONDAY | | TUESDAY | | WEDNESDAY | | THURSDAY | | FRIDAY | |
|---|---|---|---|---|---|---|---|---|---|---|
| | START | END | START | END | START | END | START | END | START | END |
| | | | | | | | | | | |
| | | | | | | | | | | |
| | | | | | | | | | | |
| | | | | | | | | | | |
| | | | | | | | | | | |
| | | | | | | | | | | |
| | | | | | | | | | | |
| | | | | | | | | | | |
| | | | | | | | | | | |
| | | | | | | | | | | |
| | | | | | | | | | | |
| | | | | | | | | | | |
| | | | | | | | | | | |

## NOTES

# HOMESCHOOL HOURS LOG BOOK

| STUDENT NAME: | | | | | | | | | | | WEEK OF: | |
|---|---|---|---|---|---|---|---|---|---|---|---|---|

| SUBJECT | MONDAY | | TUESDAY | | WEDNESDAY | | THURSDAY | | FRIDAY | |
|---|---|---|---|---|---|---|---|---|---|---|
| | START | END | START | END | START | END | START | END | START | END |
| | | | | | | | | | | |
| | | | | | | | | | | |
| | | | | | | | | | | |
| | | | | | | | | | | |
| | | | | | | | | | | |
| | | | | | | | | | | |
| | | | | | | | | | | |
| | | | | | | | | | | |
| | | | | | | | | | | |
| | | | | | | | | | | |
| | | | | | | | | | | |
| | | | | | | | | | | |
| | | | | | | | | | | |

## NOTES

# HOMESCHOOL HOURS LOG BOOK

| STUDENT NAME: | | WEEK OF: | |
|---|---|---|---|

| SUBJECT | MONDAY | | TUESDAY | | WEDNESDAY | | THURSDAY | | FRIDAY | |
|---|---|---|---|---|---|---|---|---|---|---|
| | START | END | START | END | START | END | START | END | START | END |
| | | | | | | | | | | |
| | | | | | | | | | | |
| | | | | | | | | | | |
| | | | | | | | | | | |
| | | | | | | | | | | |
| | | | | | | | | | | |
| | | | | | | | | | | |
| | | | | | | | | | | |
| | | | | | | | | | | |
| | | | | | | | | | | |
| | | | | | | | | | | |
| | | | | | | | | | | |
| | | | | | | | | | | |
| | | | | | | | | | | |

## NOTES

# HOMESCHOOL HOURS LOG BOOK

| STUDENT NAME: | | WEEK OF: | |

| SUBJECT | MONDAY | | TUESDAY | | WEDNESDAY | | THURSDAY | | FRIDAY | |
|---|---|---|---|---|---|---|---|---|---|---|
| | START | END | START | END | START | END | START | END | START | END |
| | | | | | | | | | | |
| | | | | | | | | | | |
| | | | | | | | | | | |
| | | | | | | | | | | |
| | | | | | | | | | | |
| | | | | | | | | | | |
| | | | | | | | | | | |
| | | | | | | | | | | |
| | | | | | | | | | | |
| | | | | | | | | | | |
| | | | | | | | | | | |
| | | | | | | | | | | |
| | | | | | | | | | | |

## NOTES

# HOMESCHOOL HOURS LOG BOOK

| STUDENT NAME: | | WEEK OF: | |
|---|---|---|---|

| SUBJECT | MONDAY | | TUESDAY | | WEDNESDAY | | THURSDAY | | FRIDAY | |
|---|---|---|---|---|---|---|---|---|---|---|
| | START | END | START | END | START | END | START | END | START | END |
| | | | | | | | | | | |
| | | | | | | | | | | |
| | | | | | | | | | | |
| | | | | | | | | | | |
| | | | | | | | | | | |
| | | | | | | | | | | |
| | | | | | | | | | | |
| | | | | | | | | | | |
| | | | | | | | | | | |
| | | | | | | | | | | |
| | | | | | | | | | | |
| | | | | | | | | | | |
| | | | | | | | | | | |

## NOTES

# HOMESCHOOL HOURS LOG BOOK

| STUDENT NAME: | | WEEK OF: | |
|---|---|---|---|

| SUBJECT | MONDAY | | TUESDAY | | WEDNESDAY | | THURSDAY | | FRIDAY | |
|---|---|---|---|---|---|---|---|---|---|---|
| | START | END | START | END | START | END | START | END | START | END |
| | | | | | | | | | | |
| | | | | | | | | | | |
| | | | | | | | | | | |
| | | | | | | | | | | |
| | | | | | | | | | | |
| | | | | | | | | | | |
| | | | | | | | | | | |
| | | | | | | | | | | |
| | | | | | | | | | | |
| | | | | | | | | | | |
| | | | | | | | | | | |
| | | | | | | | | | | |
| | | | | | | | | | | |

## NOTES

# HOMESCHOOL HOURS LOG BOOK

| STUDENT NAME: | | WEEK OF: | |
|---|---|---|---|

| SUBJECT | MONDAY | | TUESDAY | | WEDNESDAY | | THURSDAY | | FRIDAY | |
|---|---|---|---|---|---|---|---|---|---|---|
| | START | END | START | END | START | END | START | END | START | END |
| | | | | | | | | | | |
| | | | | | | | | | | |
| | | | | | | | | | | |
| | | | | | | | | | | |
| | | | | | | | | | | |
| | | | | | | | | | | |
| | | | | | | | | | | |
| | | | | | | | | | | |
| | | | | | | | | | | |
| | | | | | | | | | | |
| | | | | | | | | | | |
| | | | | | | | | | | |
| | | | | | | | | | | |

## NOTES

# HOMESCHOOL HOURS LOG BOOK

| STUDENT NAME: | | WEEK OF: | |
|---|---|---|---|

| SUBJECT | MONDAY | | TUESDAY | | WEDNESDAY | | THURSDAY | | FRIDAY | |
|---|---|---|---|---|---|---|---|---|---|---|
| | START | END | START | END | START | END | START | END | START | END |
| | | | | | | | | | | |
| | | | | | | | | | | |
| | | | | | | | | | | |
| | | | | | | | | | | |
| | | | | | | | | | | |
| | | | | | | | | | | |
| | | | | | | | | | | |
| | | | | | | | | | | |
| | | | | | | | | | | |
| | | | | | | | | | | |
| | | | | | | | | | | |
| | | | | | | | | | | |
| | | | | | | | | | | |

## NOTES

# HOMESCHOOL HOURS LOG BOOK

| STUDENT NAME: | | WEEK OF: | |
|---|---|---|---|

| SUBJECT | MONDAY | | TUESDAY | | WEDNESDAY | | THURSDAY | | FRIDAY | |
|---|---|---|---|---|---|---|---|---|---|---|
| | START | END | START | END | START | END | START | END | START | END |
| | | | | | | | | | | |
| | | | | | | | | | | |
| | | | | | | | | | | |
| | | | | | | | | | | |
| | | | | | | | | | | |
| | | | | | | | | | | |
| | | | | | | | | | | |
| | | | | | | | | | | |
| | | | | | | | | | | |
| | | | | | | | | | | |
| | | | | | | | | | | |
| | | | | | | | | | | |
| | | | | | | | | | | |

## NOTES

# HOMESCHOOL HOURS LOG BOOK

| STUDENT NAME: | | WEEK OF: | |

| SUBJECT | MONDAY | | TUESDAY | | WEDNESDAY | | THURSDAY | | FRIDAY | |
|---|---|---|---|---|---|---|---|---|---|---|
| | START | END | START | END | START | END | START | END | START | END |
| | | | | | | | | | | |
| | | | | | | | | | | |
| | | | | | | | | | | |
| | | | | | | | | | | |
| | | | | | | | | | | |
| | | | | | | | | | | |
| | | | | | | | | | | |
| | | | | | | | | | | |
| | | | | | | | | | | |
| | | | | | | | | | | |
| | | | | | | | | | | |
| | | | | | | | | | | |
| | | | | | | | | | | |

## NOTES

# HOMESCHOOL HOURS LOG BOOK

| STUDENT NAME: | | WEEK OF: | |
|---|---|---|---|

| SUBJECT | MONDAY | | TUESDAY | | WEDNESDAY | | THURSDAY | | FRIDAY | |
|---|---|---|---|---|---|---|---|---|---|---|
| | START | END | START | END | START | END | START | END | START | END |
| | | | | | | | | | | |
| | | | | | | | | | | |
| | | | | | | | | | | |
| | | | | | | | | | | |
| | | | | | | | | | | |
| | | | | | | | | | | |
| | | | | | | | | | | |
| | | | | | | | | | | |
| | | | | | | | | | | |
| | | | | | | | | | | |
| | | | | | | | | | | |
| | | | | | | | | | | |
| | | | | | | | | | | |

## NOTES

# HOMESCHOOL HOURS LOG BOOK

| STUDENT NAME: | | WEEK OF: | |

| SUBJECT | MONDAY | | TUESDAY | | WEDNESDAY | | THURSDAY | | FRIDAY | |
|---|---|---|---|---|---|---|---|---|---|---|
| | START | END | START | END | START | END | START | END | START | END |
| | | | | | | | | | | |
| | | | | | | | | | | |
| | | | | | | | | | | |
| | | | | | | | | | | |
| | | | | | | | | | | |
| | | | | | | | | | | |
| | | | | | | | | | | |
| | | | | | | | | | | |
| | | | | | | | | | | |
| | | | | | | | | | | |
| | | | | | | | | | | |
| | | | | | | | | | | |
| | | | | | | | | | | |

## NOTES

# HOMESCHOOL HOURS LOG BOOK

| STUDENT NAME: | | WEEK OF: | |
|---|---|---|---|

| SUBJECT | MONDAY | | TUESDAY | | WEDNESDAY | | THURSDAY | | FRIDAY | |
|---|---|---|---|---|---|---|---|---|---|---|
| | START | END | START | END | START | END | START | END | START | END |
| | | | | | | | | | | |
| | | | | | | | | | | |
| | | | | | | | | | | |
| | | | | | | | | | | |
| | | | | | | | | | | |
| | | | | | | | | | | |
| | | | | | | | | | | |
| | | | | | | | | | | |
| | | | | | | | | | | |
| | | | | | | | | | | |
| | | | | | | | | | | |
| | | | | | | | | | | |
| | | | | | | | | | | |

## NOTES

# HOMESCHOOL HOURS LOG BOOK

| STUDENT NAME: | | WEEK OF: | |
|---|---|---|---|

| SUBJECT | MONDAY | | TUESDAY | | WEDNESDAY | | THURSDAY | | FRIDAY | |
|---|---|---|---|---|---|---|---|---|---|---|
| | START | END | START | END | START | END | START | END | START | END |
| | | | | | | | | | | |
| | | | | | | | | | | |
| | | | | | | | | | | |
| | | | | | | | | | | |
| | | | | | | | | | | |
| | | | | | | | | | | |
| | | | | | | | | | | |
| | | | | | | | | | | |
| | | | | | | | | | | |
| | | | | | | | | | | |
| | | | | | | | | | | |
| | | | | | | | | | | |
| | | | | | | | | | | |

## NOTES

# HOMESCHOOL HOURS LOG BOOK

| STUDENT NAME: | | WEEK OF: | |
|---|---|---|---|

| SUBJECT | MONDAY | | TUESDAY | | WEDNESDAY | | THURSDAY | | FRIDAY | |
|---|---|---|---|---|---|---|---|---|---|---|
| | START | END | START | END | START | END | START | END | START | END |
| | | | | | | | | | | |
| | | | | | | | | | | |
| | | | | | | | | | | |
| | | | | | | | | | | |
| | | | | | | | | | | |
| | | | | | | | | | | |
| | | | | | | | | | | |
| | | | | | | | | | | |
| | | | | | | | | | | |
| | | | | | | | | | | |
| | | | | | | | | | | |
| | | | | | | | | | | |
| | | | | | | | | | | |

## NOTES

# HOMESCHOOL HOURS LOG BOOK

| STUDENT NAME: | | WEEK OF: | |
|---|---|---|---|

| SUBJECT | MONDAY | | TUESDAY | | WEDNESDAY | | THURSDAY | | FRIDAY | |
|---|---|---|---|---|---|---|---|---|---|---|
| | START | END | START | END | START | END | START | END | START | END |
| | | | | | | | | | | |
| | | | | | | | | | | |
| | | | | | | | | | | |
| | | | | | | | | | | |
| | | | | | | | | | | |
| | | | | | | | | | | |
| | | | | | | | | | | |
| | | | | | | | | | | |
| | | | | | | | | | | |
| | | | | | | | | | | |
| | | | | | | | | | | |
| | | | | | | | | | | |
| | | | | | | | | | | |

## NOTES

# HOMESCHOOL HOURS LOG BOOK

| STUDENT NAME: | | | | WEEK OF: | |
|---|---|---|---|---|---|

| SUBJECT | MONDAY | | TUESDAY | | WEDNESDAY | | THURSDAY | | FRIDAY | |
|---|---|---|---|---|---|---|---|---|---|---|
| | START | END | START | END | START | END | START | END | START | END |
| | | | | | | | | | | |
| | | | | | | | | | | |
| | | | | | | | | | | |
| | | | | | | | | | | |
| | | | | | | | | | | |
| | | | | | | | | | | |
| | | | | | | | | | | |
| | | | | | | | | | | |
| | | | | | | | | | | |
| | | | | | | | | | | |
| | | | | | | | | | | |
| | | | | | | | | | | |
| | | | | | | | | | | |

## NOTES

# HOMESCHOOL HOURS LOG BOOK

| STUDENT NAME: | | WEEK OF: | |
|---|---|---|---|

| SUBJECT | MONDAY | | TUESDAY | | WEDNESDAY | | THURSDAY | | FRIDAY | |
|---|---|---|---|---|---|---|---|---|---|---|
| | START | END | START | END | START | END | START | END | START | END |
| | | | | | | | | | | |
| | | | | | | | | | | |
| | | | | | | | | | | |
| | | | | | | | | | | |
| | | | | | | | | | | |
| | | | | | | | | | | |
| | | | | | | | | | | |
| | | | | | | | | | | |
| | | | | | | | | | | |
| | | | | | | | | | | |
| | | | | | | | | | | |
| | | | | | | | | | | |
| | | | | | | | | | | |

## NOTES

# HOMESCHOOL HOURS LOG BOOK

| STUDENT NAME: | | WEEK OF: | |
|---|---|---|---|

| SUBJECT | MONDAY | | TUESDAY | | WEDNESDAY | | THURSDAY | | FRIDAY | |
|---|---|---|---|---|---|---|---|---|---|---|
| | START | END | START | END | START | END | START | END | START | END |
| | | | | | | | | | | |
| | | | | | | | | | | |
| | | | | | | | | | | |
| | | | | | | | | | | |
| | | | | | | | | | | |
| | | | | | | | | | | |
| | | | | | | | | | | |
| | | | | | | | | | | |
| | | | | | | | | | | |
| | | | | | | | | | | |
| | | | | | | | | | | |
| | | | | | | | | | | |
| | | | | | | | | | | |

## NOTES

# HOMESCHOOL HOURS LOG BOOK

| STUDENT NAME: | | WEEK OF: | |
|---|---|---|---|

| SUBJECT | MONDAY | | TUESDAY | | WEDNESDAY | | THURSDAY | | FRIDAY | |
|---|---|---|---|---|---|---|---|---|---|---|
| | START | END | START | END | START | END | START | END | START | END |
| | | | | | | | | | | |
| | | | | | | | | | | |
| | | | | | | | | | | |
| | | | | | | | | | | |
| | | | | | | | | | | |
| | | | | | | | | | | |
| | | | | | | | | | | |
| | | | | | | | | | | |
| | | | | | | | | | | |
| | | | | | | | | | | |
| | | | | | | | | | | |
| | | | | | | | | | | |
| | | | | | | | | | | |

## NOTES

# HOMESCHOOL HOURS LOG BOOK

| STUDENT NAME: | | WEEK OF: | |
|---|---|---|---|

| SUBJECT | MONDAY | | TUESDAY | | WEDNESDAY | | THURSDAY | | FRIDAY | |
|---|---|---|---|---|---|---|---|---|---|---|
| | START | END | START | END | START | END | START | END | START | END |
| | | | | | | | | | | |
| | | | | | | | | | | |
| | | | | | | | | | | |
| | | | | | | | | | | |
| | | | | | | | | | | |
| | | | | | | | | | | |
| | | | | | | | | | | |
| | | | | | | | | | | |
| | | | | | | | | | | |
| | | | | | | | | | | |
| | | | | | | | | | | |
| | | | | | | | | | | |
| | | | | | | | | | | |
| | | | | | | | | | | |

## NOTES

# HOMESCHOOL HOURS LOG BOOK

| STUDENT NAME: | | WEEK OF: | |

| SUBJECT | MONDAY | | TUESDAY | | WEDNESDAY | | THURSDAY | | FRIDAY | |
|---|---|---|---|---|---|---|---|---|---|---|
| | START | END | START | END | START | END | START | END | START | END |
| | | | | | | | | | | |
| | | | | | | | | | | |
| | | | | | | | | | | |
| | | | | | | | | | | |
| | | | | | | | | | | |
| | | | | | | | | | | |
| | | | | | | | | | | |
| | | | | | | | | | | |
| | | | | | | | | | | |
| | | | | | | | | | | |
| | | | | | | | | | | |
| | | | | | | | | | | |
| | | | | | | | | | | |

## NOTES

# HOMESCHOOL HOURS LOG BOOK

| STUDENT NAME: | | WEEK OF: | |
|---|---|---|---|

| SUBJECT | MONDAY | | TUESDAY | | WEDNESDAY | | THURSDAY | | FRIDAY | |
|---|---|---|---|---|---|---|---|---|---|---|
| | START | END | START | END | START | END | START | END | START | END |
| | | | | | | | | | | |
| | | | | | | | | | | |
| | | | | | | | | | | |
| | | | | | | | | | | |
| | | | | | | | | | | |
| | | | | | | | | | | |
| | | | | | | | | | | |
| | | | | | | | | | | |
| | | | | | | | | | | |
| | | | | | | | | | | |
| | | | | | | | | | | |
| | | | | | | | | | | |
| | | | | | | | | | | |
| | | | | | | | | | | |

## NOTES

# HOMESCHOOL HOURS LOG BOOK

| STUDENT NAME: | | WEEK OF: | |

| SUBJECT | MONDAY | | TUESDAY | | WEDNESDAY | | THURSDAY | | FRIDAY | |
|---|---|---|---|---|---|---|---|---|---|---|
| | START | END | START | END | START | END | START | END | START | END |
| | | | | | | | | | | |
| | | | | | | | | | | |
| | | | | | | | | | | |
| | | | | | | | | | | |
| | | | | | | | | | | |
| | | | | | | | | | | |
| | | | | | | | | | | |
| | | | | | | | | | | |
| | | | | | | | | | | |
| | | | | | | | | | | |
| | | | | | | | | | | |
| | | | | | | | | | | |
| | | | | | | | | | | |

### NOTES

# HOMESCHOOL HOURS LOG BOOK

| STUDENT NAME: | | WEEK OF: | |
|---|---|---|---|

| SUBJECT | MONDAY | | TUESDAY | | WEDNESDAY | | THURSDAY | | FRIDAY | |
|---|---|---|---|---|---|---|---|---|---|---|
| | START | END | START | END | START | END | START | END | START | END |
| | | | | | | | | | | |
| | | | | | | | | | | |
| | | | | | | | | | | |
| | | | | | | | | | | |
| | | | | | | | | | | |
| | | | | | | | | | | |
| | | | | | | | | | | |
| | | | | | | | | | | |
| | | | | | | | | | | |
| | | | | | | | | | | |
| | | | | | | | | | | |
| | | | | | | | | | | |
| | | | | | | | | | | |

## NOTES

# HOMESCHOOL HOURS LOG BOOK

| STUDENT NAME: | | | | WEEK OF: | |
|---|---|---|---|---|---|

| SUBJECT | MONDAY | | TUESDAY | | WEDNESDAY | | THURSDAY | | FRIDAY | |
|---|---|---|---|---|---|---|---|---|---|---|
| | START | END | START | END | START | END | START | END | START | END |
| | | | | | | | | | | |
| | | | | | | | | | | |
| | | | | | | | | | | |
| | | | | | | | | | | |
| | | | | | | | | | | |
| | | | | | | | | | | |
| | | | | | | | | | | |
| | | | | | | | | | | |
| | | | | | | | | | | |
| | | | | | | | | | | |
| | | | | | | | | | | |
| | | | | | | | | | | |
| | | | | | | | | | | |
| | | | | | | | | | | |

## NOTES

# HOMESCHOOL HOURS LOG BOOK

| STUDENT NAME: | | WEEK OF: | |

| SUBJECT | MONDAY | | TUESDAY | | WEDNESDAY | | THURSDAY | | FRIDAY | |
|---|---|---|---|---|---|---|---|---|---|---|
| | START | END | START | END | START | END | START | END | START | END |
| | | | | | | | | | | |
| | | | | | | | | | | |
| | | | | | | | | | | |
| | | | | | | | | | | |
| | | | | | | | | | | |
| | | | | | | | | | | |
| | | | | | | | | | | |
| | | | | | | | | | | |
| | | | | | | | | | | |
| | | | | | | | | | | |
| | | | | | | | | | | |
| | | | | | | | | | | |
| | | | | | | | | | | |

## NOTES

# HOMESCHOOL HOURS LOG BOOK

| STUDENT NAME: | | WEEK OF: | |
|---|---|---|---|

| SUBJECT | MONDAY | | TUESDAY | | WEDNESDAY | | THURSDAY | | FRIDAY | |
|---|---|---|---|---|---|---|---|---|---|---|
| | START | END | START | END | START | END | START | END | START | END |
| | | | | | | | | | | |
| | | | | | | | | | | |
| | | | | | | | | | | |
| | | | | | | | | | | |
| | | | | | | | | | | |
| | | | | | | | | | | |
| | | | | | | | | | | |
| | | | | | | | | | | |
| | | | | | | | | | | |
| | | | | | | | | | | |
| | | | | | | | | | | |
| | | | | | | | | | | |
| | | | | | | | | | | |

## NOTES

# HOMESCHOOL HOURS LOG BOOK

| STUDENT NAME: | | WEEK OF: | |
|---|---|---|---|

| SUBJECT | MONDAY | | TUESDAY | | WEDNESDAY | | THURSDAY | | FRIDAY | |
|---|---|---|---|---|---|---|---|---|---|---|
| | START | END | START | END | START | END | START | END | START | END |
| | | | | | | | | | | |
| | | | | | | | | | | |
| | | | | | | | | | | |
| | | | | | | | | | | |
| | | | | | | | | | | |
| | | | | | | | | | | |
| | | | | | | | | | | |
| | | | | | | | | | | |
| | | | | | | | | | | |
| | | | | | | | | | | |
| | | | | | | | | | | |
| | | | | | | | | | | |
| | | | | | | | | | | |

## NOTES

# HOMESCHOOL HOURS LOG BOOK

| STUDENT NAME: | | WEEK OF: | |
|---|---|---|---|

| SUBJECT | MONDAY | | TUESDAY | | WEDNESDAY | | THURSDAY | | FRIDAY | |
|---|---|---|---|---|---|---|---|---|---|---|
| | START | END | START | END | START | END | START | END | START | END |
| | | | | | | | | | | |
| | | | | | | | | | | |
| | | | | | | | | | | |
| | | | | | | | | | | |
| | | | | | | | | | | |
| | | | | | | | | | | |
| | | | | | | | | | | |
| | | | | | | | | | | |
| | | | | | | | | | | |
| | | | | | | | | | | |
| | | | | | | | | | | |
| | | | | | | | | | | |
| | | | | | | | | | | |

## NOTES

www.ingramcontent.com/pod-product-compliance
Lightning Source LLC
Chambersburg PA
CBHW081311070526
44578CB00006B/834